From SHADOWS To GLIMMER

One Stroke, One Family, And The Strength To Rebuild

AISHWARYA VAIDYA

Copyright © 2025 Aishwarya Vaidya

My parents, Madhuri and Padmanabh Vaidya are my greatest inspiration and steadfast source of support. I dedicate this book to my mother, Madhuri Vaidya, who pushed me to pour my heart into these pages. This moving story is a shining example of the unbreakable bond that binds our family together, illuminating even the darkest moments of illness with utmost care and love. Through struggle and adversity, we have learned invaluable life lessons about courage and faith, discovering that true strength emerges not in the absence of hardship but in our ability to face it together.

In sharing our journey, I honor their enduring spirit and inspire others to find solace in the power of family amidst life's trials.

Prologue:

Not all battles are fought on the battlefield—some are fought in hospital rooms, in quiet prayers, and in the unwavering hands of a family refusing to give up. This gripping narrative chronicles their emotional rollercoaster as they navigate the challenges of recovery, support each other through dark moments, and ultimately emerge stronger than ever. As they confront fears and uncertainties, each family member discovers their inner strength and the true meaning of togetherness. Through moments of both silence and storms, they realize that even in the darkest corners, hope refuses to be extinguished. This motivational tale serves as an important reminder that love can heal wounds and that life's greatest battles can lead to newfound joy.

CONTENTS

Chapter 1:

<u>Golden Childhood Tales</u>

My childhood was simple, filled with laughter, love, and the kind of warmth that made home feel like the safest place on earth. In our Mumbai apartment, every corner held a story, and every moment was a lesson in love, independence, and adventure. If I was the one color-coding my books and planning every detail of my studies, Apoorva, my twin sister, was the whirlwind—losing pens, skipping homework, and somehow still charming her way through school. However, I believed in plowing my own furrow, forging my path with independence and determination.

Our parents, Madhuri and Padmanabh Vaidya, were adventurous spirits who instilled in us a love for exploration. They frequently took us on vacations, allowing us to discover new cities, immerse ourselves in different cultures, and create unforgettable memories together. These journeys not only strengthened our bond but also broadened our perspectives, teaching us valuable lessons beyond the walls of a classroom.

Like any family, we had our share of disagreements—small spats over dinner choices and the classic battle of who controlled the TV remote. Mummy and Papa always had the final say, but that never stopped Apoorva and me from trying to negotiate our way out of rules we found unfair.

Yet, no matter how intense the arguments, our home never stayed divided for long. A stern word from Papa would turn into a joke by bedtime, mummy's silent treatment would melt into a warm meal, and our sibling fights always ended with shared laughter. If there was one thing we knew for sure, it was this—love always won in our family.

Spirituality was woven into our daily lives. I remember waking up to the soft hum of mummy's prayers, the scent of incense curling through our home, and the rhythmic ringing of temple bells. My mother's devotion to Shree Swami Samartha was something we grew up watching, and in time, we embraced that faith too.

Looking back, childhood felt like a bed of roses—safe, full of love, and untouched by the storms of life. But we never know when the winds will change, and in the years ahead, we would be tested in ways we never imagined.

Chapter 2:

<u>Guided to Independence</u>

In our twenties, while many of our peers spoke excitedly about marriage and settling down, Apoorva and I were chasing something different—independence. Success, stability, and the freedom to shape our own lives came before anything else. For us, success meant more than just a paycheck—it meant proving to ourselves that we could stand on our own. There were days of self-doubt, long hours, and missed family dinners, but every milestone, no matter how small, reminded us why we chose this path.

Our parents never dictated our choices or mapped out our future—they led by example. Their lessons weren't wrapped in lectures but reflected in the way they lived, in the quiet strength of their actions. They taught us that success wasn't about following a predetermined path but about having the courage to forge our own, even if it meant stumbling along the way. They never shielded us from failure; instead, they showed us that setbacks weren't roadblocks, just stepping stones. Their belief in our ability to navigate life on our own terms was their greatest gift—a freedom that shaped not just our careers, but the very foundation of who we became.

With their guidance, we pursued our careers with determination, embracing challenges and opportunities that helped us grow. Through it all, we remained grounded in the lessons our parents had taught us—values of hard work, integrity, and self-reliance, allowing us to step into adulthood with confidence and clarity.

We were so focused on building our future that we never imagined how quickly life could change. Just when everything seemed to be falling into place, the ground beneath us shifted—and nothing would ever be the same again.

Chapter 3:

<u>Darkest Days</u>

"The Health Crisis That Turned Our World Upside Down"

September 20, 2022, started like any other day. Just two days after celebrating our mother's 60th birthday, we had no idea our world was about to collapse. At 3:00 AM, a sound shattered the night—Papa had collapsed. I was asleep in the next room when my sister woke me up. Seeing him lying on the floor overwhelmed me with shock, and I fainted—my bond with him made it hard to accept what was happening. As I began to regain consciousness, I noticed he was trying to communicate but couldn't speak clearly; this caused me to faint again. Apoorva quickly contacted our doctor, who instructed us to take my father to the hospital immediately. I was sweating bullets as my father's health took a turn for the worse. The doctors confirmed our worst fear—Papa had suffered a severe stroke, specifically a Pontine Infarct. The stroke had attacked his brainstem, the control center for movement and speech, leaving the left side of his body paralyzed. He couldn't speak. He couldn't swallow. And we had no idea if he ever would again. Our hearts sank as we came to terms with the harsh reality that his stroke was a consequence of uncontrolled diabetes that had persisted for months.

Watching him lie there, unable to communicate, was unbearable. I wanted to scream, to shake him, to make it all go away—but I could do nothing. He was trapped in his own body, and I was trapped in my helplessness.

Even though he was unable to move, he would make efforts to lift his leg and hand, despite the futility of those attempts. His hope never wavered; he was the type of person who would persist in fighting until the very end. He communicated through gestures like thumbs up and would even try to muster a smile. My mother stood as our firm support, managing everything while concealing her struggles. After five days in the hospital, my father was discharged with recommendations for intensive speech therapy and physiotherapy.

We thought the worst was over when we finally brought Papa home. But just two days later, something felt off. It started as a small hiccup—then another and another. Hours turned into a full day, and his body refused to stop. It was happening again, and this time, we had no idea why. At first, we dismissed it as something minor, assuming it would pass on its own. But as the hours stretched into days, his hiccups showed no signs of stopping, lasting for over two days without relief. Concern and confusion gripped us as we struggled to understand what was wrong.

On September 29th, we took him back to the hospital for further evaluation. The doctors conducted several assessments, but they found no significant underlying issue. After administering some medication to ease his discomfort, they discharged him within a few hours, assuring us that there was nothing serious to be concerned about. Despite this reassurance, an uneasy feeling lingered in our hearts, as we couldn't shake the sense that something deeper was at play—something we had yet to uncover.

Chapter 4:

<u>The Big Blow</u>

"When It Rains, It Pours"

It happened in seconds. One moment, Papa was resting. The next, his breath came in shallow gasps. His skin turned pale. The oxygen monitor beeped—24 mm Hg. Too low. Too dangerous. I barely had time to think before we were calling the ambulance, racing against time. In the ER, Papa suddenly started retching. His body convulsed, his face twisted in pain, and within seconds, he was vomiting uncontrollably. The doctors rushed in. Machines beeped. A mask was placed over his face. Then came the words we dreaded—aspiration pneumonia. He had inhaled food particles into his lungs, triggering a dangerous infection. The doctor informed us about Papa's condition and requested that we wait two days for a more precise assessment. He was started on tube feeding which would also need to continue at home along with catheter care.

The next 18 days blurred into hospital corridors, endless check-ups, and exhaustion so deep it felt like we were sleepwalking. Then Papa finally came home—but home didn't feel the same anymore. The bed room was now a hospital room. A feeding tube snaked from his nose. Monitors beeped softly in the background. Apoorva carefully measured his liquid meals, while Mummy and I hovered nearby, triple-checking every step. It wasn't just caregiving—it was survival, and every small mistake felt like life or death. Nights were the hardest. The silence of the house felt suffocating. Every beep of the oxygen machine in the hospital still echoed in my mind. I couldn't sleep without picturing Papa lying in that hospital bed, helpless. What if he never came back to us the same? What if he never came back at all? Yet, despite our exhaustion, we refused to give up, holding onto faith that better days would come.

I had never felt so stranded before—watching Papa suffer, unable to ease his pain, pushed me to my breaking point. It was as if I were carrying a mountain on my back, with no end in sight. His frail condition haunted me, and though I tried to hold on, I felt like a ship lost in a merciless storm. Every sleepless night chipped away at my strength, making hope seem like a fading light.

Chapter 5:

<u>The Inner Battle</u>

"I was breaking, but I refused to shatter. Some cracks ran deep, but even in my weakest moments, I held on—because love wouldn't let me fall apart completely."

I felt like I was drowning. No matter how hard I tried to keep my head above water, the weight of reality pulled me under. Every time I looked at Papa, confined to his bed, I waited for a sign that he was getting better. But days passed, and nothing changed. And that terrified me. I refused to believe this was our new reality. I still set his chair at the dining table, expecting him to come and sit like always. I caught myself listening for his voice, waiting for him to call out my name. But the house remained silent, and with each passing day, the truth became harder to ignore. It was a feeling of doom and gloom, as though the walls were closing in on me. He had always been the pillar of strength in our family, effortlessly managing everything with boundless energy. The stroke diagnosis felt impossible, almost like a cruel joke that life had played on us. The weight of this harsh reality pressed down on my chest, leading to frequent distress.

During that period, I felt quite vulnerable, struggling to cope, and in many ways, I placed my expectations on my father. I couldn't accept the reality that he was confined to bed, and I found myself being hard on both him and myself. I was down in the dumps, refusing to acknowledge the severity of the health crisis, instead clinging to hope that things would return to normal overnight. I wanted him to be the same Papa I had always known—full of energy, always on his feet, moving swiftly from one task to another without pause. I kept pushing Papa to try harder—to move his fingers, to lift his leg, to say a full sentence. 'You can do it, Papa, just try!' I would plead. But when nothing changed, frustration gnawed at me. Why wasn't he getting better? Why wasn't he fighting harder? I didn't realize then that healing wasn't about trying harder—it was about time, patience, and faith.

Collywobbles didn't surprise me anymore; my stomach was in knots every single day, and my mind filled with fear and frustration. I felt like everything was going south, spiraling into an abyss beyond my control. The sound of endless speculations from visitors and well-wishers—some hopeful, others pessimistic—only intensified my despair. My heart shattered each time someone muttered that my dad would never walk, eat, or speak independently again. I bawled my eyes out in my room, trying to drown out those words, refusing to accept that this could be our reality. I felt like I was going down in flames, burning with frustration, and helplessness. One evening, as I sat by Papa's bedside, exhausted and on the verge of tears, Apoorva placed a hand on my shoulder. 'You're not alone in this,' she whispered. Mummy sat beside me, her eyes filled with unspoken understanding. 'He will heal in his own time,' she said softly. 'But you need to heal too.' It was in that moment, with their arms around me, that I realized I wasn't just carrying Papa's pain—I was drowning in my own. And it was time to let go.

However, even in the darkest moments, one thing remained firm—our faith in Shree Swami Samartha. Alongside my mother and Apoorva, we prayed with all our hearts, holding onto his divine words—"भिऊ नकोस मी तुझ्या पाठीशी आहे" (Don't be afraid, I am with you). His blessings became our guiding force when all else seemed bleak. Our goal was clear—we wanted to see Papa walk unaided once again. That vision became our beacon of hope, something we refused to let go of, no matter how difficult the journey ahead seemed.

As the days went by, I gradually found the courage to embrace this new reality. It wasn't easy, but I forced myself to step out of my despair and focus on what truly mattered—being a source of strength for Papa, not another weight for him to carry. Strength isn't about never breaking—it's about picking up the pieces and moving forward. I had spent so long trying to be strong for Papa that I forgot healing wasn't just for him—it was for all of us. And that meant learning to let go of control, to trust the process, and to believe that even in the darkest moments, we were never truly alone. I had to get my act together, not just for myself, but for him. I held on to the belief that even in the darkest tunnels, there is always a glimmer of light ahead.

Papa often teased me about being overly sensitive compared to the rebel, strong-willed Aishwarya he knew. Yet, my heartfelt words nearly brought him to tears as I reassured him: "Papa, it's perfectly fine to feel weak or sensitive; it's okay to cry or express emotions. I'm not ashamed of being seen as weak at times because everyone has their moments of vulnerability but quitting is not an option. My concern stemmed from a deep love for you that shook me profoundly; the thought of losing you was unbearable. You are my superhero, my support system, my guiding light amid chaos. In my eyes, you have always been a protector, so how could I bear witness to your struggles with walking, eating, sitting, or even speaking?"

That day, for the first time in a long while, I saw Papa's eyes glisten. He looked at me, his lips trembling, as if trying to find the right words—but none came. Mummy, too, couldn't hold back. Silent tears ran down her cheeks as she pulled me into a tight embrace. She didn't say a word, but in that moment, her arms told me everything—we were in this together. No matter how painful this journey was, we would find our way through it, together. That moment changed something within me. It was a reminder that even in our darkest times, love, faith, and resilience could light the way forward.

Chapter 6

Finding Light Again

"The Darkest Hour Is Just Before Dawn"

The darkest nights had passed, and dawn had finally arrived. Papa's health was improving—slowly, but surely. The weight that had pressed down on our hearts for months began to lift, and for the first time in a long while, we could breathe again. Hope had returned, and with it, the promise of better days ahead. Physiotherapy and speech therapy were ongoing, as our primary goal was to help Papa regain his ability to stand and walk independently again. Despite the physical strain and emotional exhaustion, he was determined. From the very beginning, his only wish was to get out of bed and reclaim his mobility—he refused to let his condition define him. No setback discouraged him; he faced every challenge head-on, fueled by an unshakable will to recover. Papa would often say, no matter what, "Keep your chin up."

Three months of limitless efforts led to this moment. Papa began taking small steps on his own, a moment that filled us with immense joy and hope. Tears blurred my vision as I realized—we were witnessing a miracle in motion. After months of waiting, hoping, and praying, Papa was walking again. His spirit was remarkable—he pushed himself beyond his limits, never once complaining, never once giving up. His perseverance paid off, and soon both the feeding tube and catheter were removed.

For months, I had dreamed of one simple thing—coming home to find Papa standing at the door, just as he always had before. That day finally came. As I walked toward the house, my heart pounded. The door creaked open, and there he was—standing, smiling, waiting for me. My breath caught in my throat. I ran to him, barely able to contain my tears. 'You did it, Papa,' I whispered, gripping his hands. He simply smiled, as if he had never doubted this moment would come. And in that instant, I knew—we had won this battle. It was a moment of triumph, one that filled my heart with overwhelming gratitude and relief. I rejoiced, knowing how much strength and grit it had taken to reach this point. Turning to mummy and Apoorva, I congratulated them for the endless efforts. It felt like a shared victory—one that proved the power of care, and faith.

As a family, we did everything possible to support his recovery, but it was Papa's spirit that truly made the difference. He was relentless in his pursuit of normalcy, never allowing frustration to overpower his resolve. With a smile on his face and a positive attitude, he resumed eating, transitioning from semi-solids to regular food, and soon, he could speak clearly again.

By December 2022, he was walking unaided again, and by January 2023, he had regained full independence, just as he had before his illness.

Papa embraced his daily routine with enthusiasm, going for walks, managing his chores, and proving to everyone that his willpower was stronger than any obstacle life had thrown his way. His recovery was not just a testimony to medical care but to the incredible power of the human spirit—the sheer force of will that refuses to surrender.

Papa adhered to all the doctor's guidelines with discipline, following his prescribed diet and exercise routine meticulously. He never skipped a meal plan, carefully monitored his intake, and ensured that he engaged in the recommended physiotherapy and mobility exercises. His commitment to recovery was evident in every effort he made, and as each day passed, we saw gradual but promising improvements.

Papa seemed to be getting better over months, and as a family, we began to breathe easier, believing that the worst was behind us. The long and difficult days of uncertainty seemed to be fading into the past, replaced by a newfound optimism. We had fought tirelessly alongside him, providing our constant support, and we felt as though we had triumphed in our struggle. It felt like we had won the battle, emerging stronger and more resilient than before.

We thought we had won. That we had fought the hardest battle and emerged stronger than ever. But fate had other plans. Just as we began to believe the worst was behind us, a new storm gathered on the horizon—one we never saw coming, one that would shake us to our core.

Chapter 7:

<u>The Stroke Returns</u>

On December 20, 2023, another wave of devastation crashed into our lives. That morning, Mummy suddenly began vomiting and appeared disoriented. At first, we clung to hope. Maybe it was just acidity. Maybe she was just exhausted. But deep down, a terrible fear stirred. We had been here before. The way her pupils dilated, the way confusion clouded her eyes—it was a nightmare on repeat. And this time, we knew exactly what it meant. Without wasting a second, we rushed her to the hospital, our hearts pounding with dread.

An MRI confirmed our worst fear— Mummy had suffered a stroke. The words hit us like a ton of bricks. Though she was promptly admitted and recovered well enough to be discharged after three days, a lingering anxiety concerned us. It felt like we were stuck in a vicious cycle, one where just as we regained our footing, the ground was yanked from beneath us again.

Life was playing a cruel joke on us. Just six days later, on December 26, 2023, Mummy began vomiting again. The air shifted. My stomach knotted. No, no, no. Not again. I looked at Apoorva, and in her eyes, I saw the same silent horror. We didn't wait this time. We grabbed our bags, rushed her to the hospital, and prayed that history wasn't repeating itself. But fate had dealt us another cruel blow—this time, it was a major stroke. It felt like déjà vu, but this time, the storm was fiercer, the battle much harder.

Apoorva and I sat in the dim hospital corridor, numb with exhaustion. The weight of reality pressed down on us like an invisible force, suffocating, unrelenting. We knew this feeling too well—the helplessness, the fear, and the aching uncertainty. And yet, no matter how many times life had tested us, it never got easier. We felt like we were walking on eggshells, afraid that any moment could bring another heartbreak. Tears streamed down our faces as we clung to each other for comfort, seeking solace in the shared pain that words alone could not express. It was as if a dark cloud had settled over us, refusing to lift. Then, a thought pierced through the fog of our grief. We had been here before. We had survived before. And if we had learned anything from Papa's journey, it was this—strength is a choice. When the going gets tough, the tough get going. We wiped our tears and made a silent promise: We would not let this break us. We would fight for Mummy the way she had always fought for us and do whatever it took to bring Mummy home again.

We threw ourselves into action—consulting doctors tirelessly, researching treatment options, and staying by her side day and night. Every decision mattered. Every moment counted. When doctors hesitated, we demanded answers. When options seemed limited, we searched for alternatives. We became her voice when she couldn't speak, her strength when she was too weak to fight. Failure was not an option. The battle was exhausting, both emotionally and physically, but we knew that 'Fortune Favors The Brave', and we had no choice but to be brave for Mummy.

As the days passed, we found strength not just in our love for her but also in our deepened bond as a family. We clung to that hope, believing that despite the storm, the sun would shine again. Mummy had always been our anchor, the heart of our home, and now, it was our turn to be hers. No matter how tough or uncertain the road ahead was, we were committed to doing everything possible to help her regain her strength and return to her normal life.

Despite being a stroke survivor himself, Papa never wavered. He spent long hours by Mummy's side at the hospital while also managing household responsibilities and finances, proving once again that his strength knew no bounds. Together, we held each other up, refusing to let the weight of this battle crush us. And on January 3, 2024, we finally brought Mummy home.

Chapter 8:

<u>Conquering Stroke</u>

Mummy was home, but she wasn't the same. She sat in silence, staring at the floor, her hands clasped tightly in her lap. The warmth in her eyes had dimmed, replaced by something unfamiliar—self-doubt. 'I've become a burden,' she whispered one evening, her voice barely audible. Guilt weighed heavily on her, and she often voiced her sorrow, apologizing repeatedly for what she believed was the trouble she had caused Apoorva, Papa, and me. The words crushed me. How could she not see what we saw? How could she not realize she was the heart of our home, the force that held us together?

Nothing could ever overshadow the deep, unbreakable bond we share with our parents. They are like the roots of a mighty tree, anchoring us in every storm and giving us the strength to stand tall. Just as they had spent their entire lives nurturing and protecting us, it was now our turn to ensure Mummy's comfort, care, and recovery.

Apoorva and I devoted ourselves entirely to Mummy's well-being. I made sure her medicines were taken on time, while Apoorva sat by her side, patiently feeding her spoonfuls of warm dal-chawal. On difficult nights, we would hold her hands, whispering stories of childhood mischief to make her smile. Slowly, the sadness in her eyes began to fade. Love has a way of healing, and we were determined to remind her of that. We took turns staying by her side, learning every detail of her treatment plan, speaking to doctors, and adjusting her routine to help her regain strength. The nights were long and often sleepless, but we didn't mind. Love knows no fatigue when it comes to family.

Papa, despite his own struggles, refused to let Mummy lose hope. 'I may have survived a stroke, but you're the real fighter,' he teased one afternoon, nudging her playfully. She tried to glare at him but failed—because she was laughing. It was the first real laugh we had heard in weeks. In that moment, I knew—Papa wasn't just helping Mummy heal; he was bringing her back to life.

Apoorva and I took turns playing indoor games with her, keeping her engaged and distracted from negative thoughts. We celebrated even the smallest of victories—finishing a full meal, or even simply smiling after a rough day. Slowly but surely, she began to believe in herself again. Faith moves mountains, and our belief in Shree Swami Samartha never wavered. His blessings and miracles continued to guide us. Every prayer, every chant, and every offering of gratitude strengthened our belief that Mummy would heal, and indeed, day by day, she showed remarkable progress.

Though the journey was far from easy, we refused to give up. We stood as one, knowing that together, as a family, we could fight any battle. With love, patience, faith, and sheer determination, we would help Mummy not just recover, but regain the confidence and joy that had always defined her.

Chapter 9:

<u>Rising Like a Phoenix</u>

"Daughters Can Do It All"

Apoorva and I never imagined we would have to become caregivers overnight. One moment, we were daughters, relying on our parents for guidance. The next, we were their pillars, their protectors. When both our parents suffered strokes, life turned into an uphill battle, testing our patience, endurance, and emotional strength. But if there was one thing we had learned from them, it was this—when life knocks you down, you rise stronger. Instead of crumbling under the pressure, we grabbed the bull by the horns and faced each challenge head-on.

Our parents had always been the wind beneath our wings, lifting us through every storm. They had devoted their lives to our happiness, always putting us first. Now, it was our turn to stand tall as their support system. Apoorva and I, but we refused to falter. We were taught by our parents that "love and care can work wonders even in the darkest times".

"Our parents are our support system," Apoorva reflected. "Now, it was time for us to hold them up, no matter what it took."

We strongly believed that "a little spark can ignite a great fire," and with that in mind, we committed ourselves to their healing journey. We vowed to turn every stumbling block into a stepping stone, every setback into a setup for a comeback.

It was important for us to turn every mess into a message, every test into a testimony, and every experience into a lesson.

Balancing work, household duties, and caregiving felt like walking a tightrope with no safety net. We took shifts at the hospital, handled calls with doctors, and still made sure dinner was on the table at home. Sleep became a luxury we couldn't afford. But we refused to let exhaustion break us. Some nights, Apoorva and I would collapse onto the couch, staring at each other, knowing we had to wake up and do it all over again. But we held on, knowing that every sacrifice, every sleepless night, brought us one step closer to seeing our parents heal. From coordinating treatments to lifting their spirits, we left no stone unturned. We became their caretakers, motivators, and most importantly, their source of hope.

But this journey wasn't just about their physical recovery—it was about breathing life back into their world. Seeing our parents rediscover joy and confidence became our greatest reward. No matter how drained we felt, their smallest victories fueled our determination to push forward.

Apoorva and I worked day and night, ensuring that love, patience, and warmth filled every moment of their recovery. It was in those moments that we truly realized the depth of our bond as a family. They built our world with love; now, we are rebuilding theirs with the same devotion.

This journey proved what we had always known—family is not just about blood, but about standing by each other through thick and thin. We had walked through fire, but instead of being consumed by it, we emerged like a phoenix rising from the ashes, stronger than ever. We were not just daughters fulfilling a duty—we were warriors, forged in fire, standing unshaken even in the fiercest storms. Pain had tested us, uncertainty had threatened to break us, but we refused to yield. We had carried our parents through their darkest hours, but in doing so, we had also discovered our own strength—the kind of strength that doesn't just endure but rises, unbreakable, against all odds. Daughters don't just support; they lead, they fight, and they conquer. I wouldn't say that we have weathered the storm, but we have certainly learned to stand strong and face it with courage.

Chapter 10:

<u>Life After Stroke: A Stronger Bond</u>

The weight of possibly losing both our parents bore down on us, yet we were determined to move mountains if that's what it took to bring them back to good health. Papa has made remarkable progress and is thriving once again. More than a year after Mummy's stroke, with prompt medical care and diligent follow-ups, she has regained her independence. She now finds joy in taking walks with Papa, rekindling her social life, and returning to her beloved kitchen, reclaiming the rhythm of daily life.

For months, our home had felt more like a hospital—filled with medicine schedules, whispered prayers, and sleepless nights. Now, laughter echoed in its halls again. Our family had been through fire and brimstone, but instead of falling apart, we emerged stronger, bound by an unshakable resilience. The saying holds: 'A House Divided Against Itself Cannot Stand'. We realized that facing these challenges together was far easier than struggling in isolation. Through trials and tribulations, we have forged deeper connections, reinforcing our foundation as a family.

That's not to say life is now smooth sailing. Like any family, we still have our fair share of disagreements and hurdles, but we have learned to meet each other halfway, communicate with open hearts, and find common ground. Our time together has become sacred—we seize every opportunity to strengthen our bond. Weekends are no longer just days off; they are reserved for quality time, laughter, and shared experiences. We break bread as a family whenever possible, engaging in lively conversations over meals. Our home is once again filled with music—Papa tapping his feet to an old Bollywood classic, Apoorva twirling him around as Mummy and I burst into laughter. Our evening strolls aren't just walks; they are conversations, memories in motion, and reminders of all we fought for. And when we gather for a meal, it isn't just food—it's a celebration of togetherness, a moment of gratitude for what we nearly lost.

With our hectic weekday schedules, sitting down for meals together isn't always feasible. However, we have carved out a simple yet meaningful tradition—no matter how busy the day gets, we ensure that at least half an hour before bedtime is spent reconnecting, sharing stories, and reflecting on the day gone by. These small moments, woven together, remind us that though life may throw curveballs, love, unity, and resilience will always see us through.

This is simply our story—not extraordinary, nor unique in its struggles, as countless others face similar or even greater challenges—but it is ours. The journey we've been on, shaped by both hardships and hope, has taught us lessons we might not have learned otherwise. It has strengthened us, molding us into individuals capable of confronting life's difficulties head-on.

Overcoming the challenges of a stroke was no small feat, but it gave us the courage and belief that we can tackle whatever life throws our way. Bring it on! We're prepared for any challenges that lie ahead, bolstered by the lessons we've learned and the strength we've found in each other.

We remain hopeful for success because giving up is not an option we will consider. Instead, we've chosen to embrace every struggle, and every battle, with faith and determination. Through it all, we express our heartfelt gratitude to Shree Swami Samartha, whose blessings have been our guiding light and supported us in moments of despair, turning what once seemed impossible into reality. Life tested us in ways we never expected, but it also showed us the power of love, faith, and family. We may not know what lies ahead, but one thing is certain—whatever comes next, we will face it together, hand in hand, just like we always have.

As we step forward, carrying the lessons of resilience, love, and faith, one thing remains certain—the strongest steel is forged in the hottest fire.

Chapter 11:

<u>Healing Together</u>

When both our parents suffered strokes, we had no roadmap—we learned everything through trial and error. There were moments of exhaustion, moments of doubt, but through it all, we discovered what truly helps a family heal. If there's one thing we've learned, it's this—facing a stroke in the family is never easy, but with the right mindset and approach, it can be navigated with resilience and hope. Here are some tips for families to manage this difficult time:

Embrace unity: Lean on each other for support. A strong family bond can provide emotional stability and help lighten the burden. Share responsibilities and maintain open communication to ensure everyone feels involved and valued.

Educate yourself: Learn about stroke and its effects. Understanding the condition, treatment options and rehabilitation processes helps you make informed decisions and support recovery effectively.

Create a positive environment: Love and encouragement play a significant role in healing. Celebrate small victories, stay patient, and infuse optimism into daily interactions to boost the morale of the recovering individual.

Prioritize self-care: Caregiving can be physically and emotionally draining. Take time to rest and recharge. A healthy caregiver is vital to the recovery process.

Be determined and hopeful: Recovery takes time and effort. Approach each day with determination and maintain hope. Progress may be slow, but persistence pays off.

Seek Professional Help: don't hesitate to consult therapists and doctors. Joining support groups can also provide valuable insights and emotional support.

Together, families can turn lemons into lemonade, proving that every cloud has a silver lining. Love is the anchor that steadies a family through the fiercest storms. When life tested us, we didn't just survive—we grew stronger, closer, and more resilient. Because in the end, it's not just about overcoming hardships; it's about discovering the depth of love that carries us through them.

Life Continues, Keep Hustling!

What happens when life changes in an instant? When the people who have always been your strength suddenly need you to be theirs? This is the story of the Vaidya family—a journey of heartbreak, resilience, and unwavering love. When both parents suffer debilitating strokes in quick succession, their world is turned upside down. Faced with fear, uncertainty, and the daunting challenges of recovery, the family must rally together like never before. Through heart-wrenching moments and inspiring perseverance, this poignant narrative highlights the strength of love and unity in overcoming hardships. From long nights in hospital corridors to moments of quiet strength at home, each family member plays a crucial role—learning, adapting, and finding courage in unexpected places. They face setbacks, small victories, and the unrelenting fear of the unknown, but through it all, they discover a resilience they never knew they possessed. With raw honesty and uplifting moments, this story showcases how hope can shine through even in our darkest times.

Rebuilding After the Storm

For the longest time, I believed that fighting the battle was the hardest part—but I soon realized that what came after was just as challenging. Survival isn't the finish line; healing is.

After everything my family endured, I expected life to return to normal. But what even was "normal" anymore? The anxiety, the emotional exhaustion, the constant fear of what could go wrong—it didn't disappear just because things started to get better. Healing wasn't automatic. It was a choice I had to make every single day.

So, I started small. I wrote. I poured my tangled emotions onto paper, untangling them word by word. Journaling became my safe space, a place to process the grief, the hope, the fears, and everything in between.

I turned to self-care, not as an afterthought, but as a necessity. Fitness became more than just exercise—it was an anchor, a way to clear my mind, to remind myself that strength wasn't just emotional, but physical too. Mindfulness taught me to stop living in the "what ifs" of the past and future, and instead embrace the present moment, fully and completely.

Through this journey, I also realized something I had never given much thought to before: we take far too much for granted—our health, our family, our time. It's easy to assume there's always more of it, until suddenly, you're faced with the reality that life is fragile, and everything you love can change in an instant.

Slowly, I transformed. The anxiety loosened its grip. The past no longer controlled me. I became self-aware, present, stronger. I replaced self-doubt with gratitude, fear with faith, exhaustion with purpose. I stopped waiting for life to "go back to normal" and started creating a new version of normal—one built on intention, love, and a deep appreciation for the things that truly matter.

This journey changed me—but I chose how it changed me.

"If there's one thing I've learned, it's this: we don't always get to choose what happens to us, but we always get to choose how we respond. Life continues, and so must we. Healing is never a straight path, and neither is growth. But no matter how many times we stumble, we always have the power to rise again—stronger, wiser, and more alive than ever before."

Afterword

To the families who have faced their battles—those who have sat in waiting rooms, held trembling hands, whispered silent prayers—may this book remind you that even in the darkest moments, there is light to be found in love, hope, and unity. The emotional highs and lows depicted in this tale mirror the realities many of us encounter, but they also illuminate the extraordinary capacity of the human spirit to heal and rebuild.

This narrative is dedicated to those who refuse to give up, who find strength in vulnerability, and who remind us that life's greatest victories are not measured by what we achieve alone but by the bonds we nurture along the way.

As I reflect on this journey—every fear, every triumph, every moment of doubt—I realize that strength is not about never falling but about rising every single time. And if this story has touched even one heart, reminded one person that they are not alone, then every word has been worth it. Thank you for joining this family on their journey. May their story remind you to hold your loved ones a little closer, to embrace resilience in the face of uncertainty, and to seek joy even in the smallest moments. Because even after the longest night, the sun will rise again—and so will you.

<u>Acknowledgments</u>

Every step I take, every word I write, carries the imprint of my parents' love and wisdom. They are the reason I stand strong today, their unwavering belief in me shaping not just my successes, but the very essence of who I am. This book is as much theirs as it is mine—a reflection of the lessons they've taught, the love they've given, and the resilience they've instilled in me.

I owe every milestone, every accomplishment, and every step forward to the foundation they have built for me. Mom and Dad, you are my inspiration and my pillars of strength. I carry your lessons and love with me in everything I do, and I am grateful for the incredible parents you are.

Kudos to my sister Apoorva, my co-pilot through every storm. There were nights when exhaustion threatened to consume us, yet she never faltered. Whether it was handling the hardest medical decisions or simply holding my hand when words failed, she was my rock. Apoorva, you are not just my sister—you are my strength, my mirror, and my greatest ally in life. Her ability to remain calm under pressure, and offer support without reserve, speaks volumes about her dedication.

Apoorva, you truly are a force to be reckoned with, and we are beyond proud and grateful to have you by our side. Thank you for being our anchor, our cheerleader, and our support system.

Deepest gratitude to Anand Vaidya, Ann Vaidya, Suchitra Shete, Nikhil Khopkar, Rohan Khopkar, Anita Khopkar, Amita Patkar, Gautam Patkar, and the Narvekar family (Neha, Sunil, Karan, and Jyoti) for their support and kindness during the most challenging times of our lives.

Your presence, encouragement, and acts of love provided us with the strength to navigate through the darkest moments. Whether it was through your comforting words, lending a helping hand, or simply being there when we needed you the most, your steadfast support has been critical for our family.

Each of you has played an irreplaceable role, reminding us of the power of togetherness. Your compassion and empathy have left an indelible mark on our hearts, and we feel truly blessed to have such incredible individuals standing by our side. You are not just friends and family; you are our pillars of strength, and we will forever be grateful for your presence in our lives.

To my incredible mains- Aishwarya Iyer, Somita Pal, Priyanka Domse, Gargi Parab, and Apurva Sawant, you have shown me the true meaning of friendship in the most profound and beautiful way.

Through every twist and turn, every high and low, you have stood by my side, offering not just your support but your unconditional love and faith in me. You've celebrated my victories as if they were your own and lifted me during my hardest moments, never letting me feel alone. Each of you has been my rock, my confidante, and my cheerleader, and I am endlessly grateful for the bond we share.

Your belief in me has been my driving force, helped me to keep pushing forward even when the road seemed impossible. You have been there through the laughter, the tears, the chaos, and the quiet, proving time and time again that true friendship isn't just about being present during the good times; it's about holding space for each other during the hardest ones.

I am delighted to have each of you in my life. You've shown me the beauty of connection, the strength of standing together, and the magic of knowing that no matter what, I have an unshakable circle of love and support. Thank you for being my family in every way that matters. You are my heart, and my forever tribe, and I cherish you more than words can ever express.

I am deeply grateful to my cousin sister, Dr. Smita Harsha, for her invaluable guidance, and relentless follow-ups throughout this journey. Her expertise, compassion, and constant encouragement provided us with reassurance and clarity during the most challenging times. We couldn't have navigated this path without her thoughtful advice.

To Komal Ambare, Sonali Kadam, Archana Iyer, Kirti Rele, Upneet Pansare, Harsha Advani Kanal, and Vinodini Krishnakumar, thank you for always checking in on me and ensuring I was doing well.

Ameya Khopkar has played a crucial role in our lives, taking it upon himself to ensure that we never had to worry about essentials, meticulously managing our food and medication needs. He also made sure that our parents received the best possible care. His presence brought us reassurance, allowing us to focus on their recovery without the added burden of these responsibilities. His kindness, dedication, and selflessness made an immense difference in our experience.

I extend my deepest appreciation to Dr. Sucheta Dhuri, Devaki Didi whose guidance has been invaluable. A sincere thank you to Pravin Taparia, Ajaya Taparia, Jatin Deshpande, Asmita Deshpande, Vinod Khopkar, Swati Khopkar, Ravindra Khopkar, Achyut Vaidya, Dusange family (Supriya, Sudhir, Mahesh, Nancy), Shirish Shete, and Sameer for their assistance.

I am deeply thankful to Nakul Patil, Neha Patil, and Aniruddha Kamble for their help with medication supplies and other essential needs.

A special mention goes to Nagesh Naik (Tejas), a true cancer warrior whose journey has been a source of immense inspiration. His courage and resilience motivated me to write for the first time, and his book, **The Butterfly Breaks Free: A Bulletproof Transformation Journey of a Cancer Survivor**, is a testimony to his strength and spirit. I encourage everyone to read this remarkable story of triumph over adversity. Kindly visit his website- https://www.nageshnaik.com for the latest updates.

I also want to Gloocal Communications Pvt. Ltd., including Parag Dhurke, Bhaskar Tare, and Nikita Kamdar, for allowing me to thrive even during challenging times.

I express my heartfelt gratitude to the medical professionals whose dedication, expertise, and compassion ensured that my parents maintained excellent health throughout challenging times. Their relentless efforts to provide the highest quality of care made all the difference, and we remain deeply indebted to them.

My sincere thanks go to Gleneagles Hospitals, Parel, Mumbai, including Dr. Pankaj Agarwal, Dr. Manjusha Agarwal, Dr. Ameet Mandot, Dr. Nitin Dange, and his team as each of them played a pivotal role in not only addressing the medical challenges but also ensuring that my parents felt supported, valued, and cared for every step of the way. Their skillful hands and kind hearts brought comfort and healing during moments of uncertainty. The warmth and reassurance they provided went beyond their professional duties, demonstrating their genuine care for the well-being of my parents.

Thank you Jaitali Bandarkar, Unnati Shelar, and Dr. Yash Junnarkar. Each of you brought your unique expertise, empathy, and kindness to every interaction, making my parents feel not just cared for but truly valued. Whether it was through your prompt instructions or comforting presence, you consistently went the extra mile, and it never went unnoticed.

A shout-out to the incredibly talented Vidya Shinde, who has been by my side despite us knowing each other for just a year. As a millennial, I feel fortunate to have a Gen Z friend like her who has not only brought fresh perspectives into my life but has also helped keep the child in me alive with her infectious energy and zest for life.

Vidya's passion went beyond words when it came to supporting me with my book. She didn't just contribute her unique ideas; she treated the book—my labor of love, my child—with as much care, devotion, and pride as I did. Vidya, your kindness, creativity, and camaraderie have been a gift I will cherish forever.

I want to thank everyone who has played a role in our journey, no matter how big or small. This journey has been made brighter and more hopeful because of each one of you.

www.ingramcontent.com/pod-product-compliance
Lightning Source LLC
Chambersburg PA
CBHW020652160726
47991CB00003B/1152